Making Music

Blowing

Angela Aylmore

Raintree

Chicago, Illinois

© 2006 Raintree
Published by Raintree, a division of Reed Elsevier, Inc.
Chicago, Illinois
Customer Service 888-363-4266
Visit our website at www.raintreelibrary.com

Printed and bound by South China Printing Company.
10 09 08 07 06
10 9 8 7 6 5 4 3 2 1

Library of Congress Cataloging-in-Publication Data:

Aylmore, Angela.
  Blowing / Angela Aylmore.
      p. cm. -- (Making music)
  Includes indexes.
  ISBN 1-4109-1605-7 (library binding-hardcover) -- ISBN 1-4109-1610-3
(pbk.) 1. Wind instruments--Juvenile literature. 1. Title. 11. Series: Aylmore,
Angela. Making music.
  ML930.A94 2005
  788'.19--dc22

                                        2005002424

Acknowledgments
The publishers would like to thank the following for permission to reproduce photographs:
Alamy pp. **15**, **16**; Corbis pp. **5a**, **13**, **17**, **18**; Getty Images p. **14** (photodisc); Harcourt Education pp. **4a** (Trevor Clifford), **5a**, **5b**, **6**, **7**, **8**, **9**, **10a**, **10b**, **11**, **12**, **19**, **20**, **21**, **22-23** (Tudor Photography).

Cover photograph of a boy playing a trumpet, reproduced with permission of Tudor Photography/ Harcourt Education.

Some words are shown in bold, **like this**. You can find out what they mean by looking in the glossary on page 24.

Contents

Let's Make Music!

We can make **music** by blowing!

Nia is playing her recorder.

Blow the harmonica!

zoo-zoo-zoo

4

Toot, toot goes the trumpet!

Hear the panpipes.

whoo, whoo!

Play the Recorder

Can you play the recorder?

Blow it gently.
Make a soft **note**.

Blow it hard.
Make a
loud note.

Long and Short

Play some short **notes**.

peep
peep
peep
peep

Make Your Own

Can you make an **instrument** to blow?

Use a bottle and some water.

Blow your bottle.

Make a sound!

Sounds Like...

Listen to the whistle.
What could it be?

12

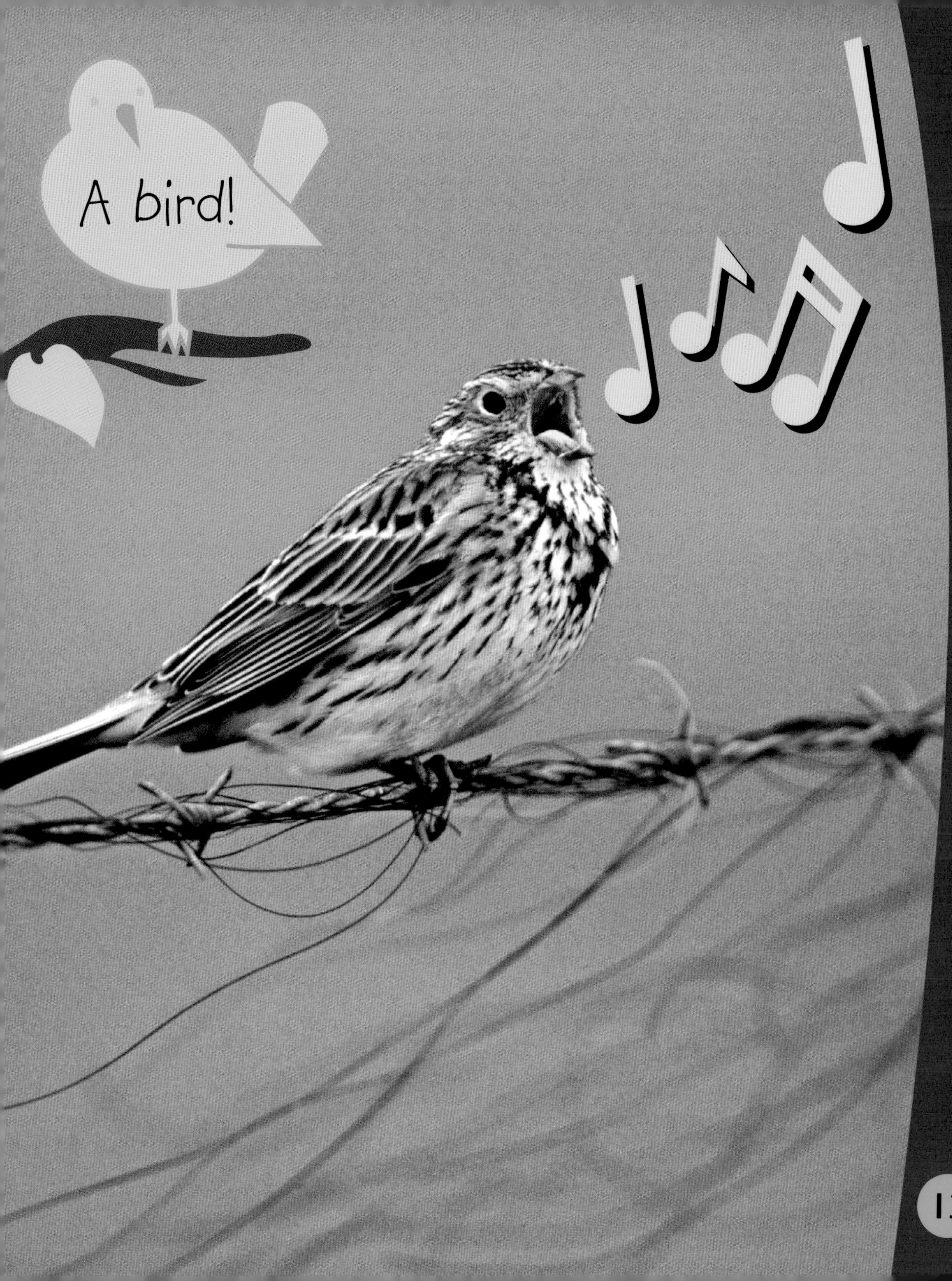

A bird!

High and Low

This is
a flute.

The flute makes a soft high so[...]

This is a big tuba!

The tuba makes a deep and low sound.

What Is It?

This is a shofar.
It comes from Israel.

It is made
from a
ram's horn.

Can you play a horn?

Fingers and Feet

Fingers that go up and down.
Feet that march around.

Can you make a marching band?

right

left

right

left

left

March in time to the **music!**

Listen Carefully

What can you hear?

What makes that sound?

recorder

maracas

violin

triangle

It's the recorder!

All Together Now!

whoo
whoo

toot
toot

Let's all play together!

peep

peep

trr trr

Glossary

instrument an object that can produce musical sounds

music a mixture of sounds to express an idea or emotion

notes a specific single sound, which can be written

Index

Notes for Adults

Making Music provides children with an opportunity to think about sound and the different ways instruments can be played to create music. The concept of volume, rhythm, speed, and pitch are introduced, and children are encouraged to think about how controlling their movements can create different sounds when they play instruments.

This book looks at different ways of creating music by blowing. It covers different instruments that can be blown and the type of sounds that they make. Children are encouraged to think about how to play quickly, slowly, loudly, and quietly.

Follow-up activities

• Using a recorder, or similar instrument, play two notes for the children. Ask them to identify whether the second note was higher or lower than the first.

• Play the children an example of a piece of music, such as Peter and the Wolf by Sergei Prokofiev. Can they pick out any instruments that sound like they are blown to create music?

Aylmore, Angela.

788
AYL

Blowing /

jj8314